Pepsi-Cola Collectibles

With Price Guide

EVERETTE & MARY Lloyd

Schiffer Publishing Ltd

77 Lower Valley Road, Atglen, PA 19310

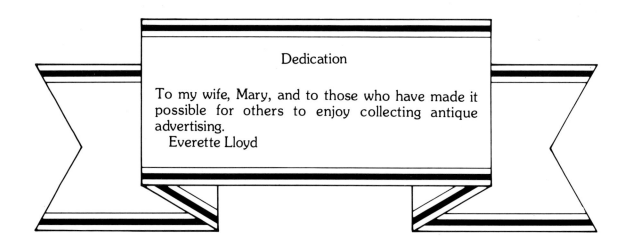

Dedication

To my wife, Mary, and to those who have made it possible for others to enjoy collecting antique advertising.
    Everette Lloyd

Designed by Bonnie Hensley

Printed in the United States of America.
ISBN: 0-88740-533-9

Published by Schiffer Publishing, Ltd.
77 Lower Valley Road
Atglen, PA 19310
Please write for a free catalog.
This book may be purchased from the publisher.
Please include $2.95 postage.
Try your bookstore first.

We are interested in hearing from authors with book ideas on related subjects.

Contents

A kaleidoscope can from 1981.

Acknowledgements

The Everette Lloyd family and Schiffer Publishing would like to thank Gary Metz, a noted collector of memorabilia and owner of the Muddy River Trading Company in Roanoke, Virginia, for his contributions to this project.

Gary carefully organized and catalogued the collection for auction last year. Credit for a successful auction belongs entirely to him. His technical contribution to Schiffer Publishing is apparent by the enclosed price guide and his assistance in photographing and preparing the collection for publication.

Gary's interest and support made the auction of the Everette Lloyd Collection and the publication of this book possible.

Mary Lloyd
Hillsborough, NC

Preface

Pepsi Cola has always been a big part of our family. It's been our soft drink of choice as long as we can remember, and its advertising has dominated both dinner conversation and the walls of our home for years.

Our dad was an avid collector of many things his entire life, but nothing compared to his interest in Pepsi-Cola memorabilia. Since Pepsi originated "down the road" in New Bern, he took pride in the fact that Pepsi was a "local" creation. Also, Daddy's interest was piqued because Pepsi memorabilia was rare and difficult to find. Pepsi was his passion and his obsession and was truly one of the great joys of his life. He was naturally gregarious and cherished the friendships he made through his Pepsi collecting as much as the advertising memorabilia itself. Our family—and I'm sure many of you—have wonderful anecdotes about and memories of him as a collector and as a person.

The publication of this book on our father's Pepsi-Cola collection realizes a long-standing dream. At the time of his death, our dad was in the process of planning this book and making arrangements for its publication. At that time, there were no other guides to Pepsi-Cola memorabilia available. It was his fondest dream to publish such a guide for Pepsi collectors, and it is with great pride that we, along with Schiffer Publishing, offer "Pepsi Cola Collectibles" to Pepsi lovers everywhere.

Our dad planned to dedicate his book to his wife and our mother, Mary, and we would like that dedication to stand. She enabled him to collect Pepsi memorabilia to his heart's desire by minding the family business and keeping our home and family intact. She also made sure that the best and most cherished Pepsi items Daddy brought home were beautifully framed and tastefully hung in the family den. This book would not be complete without that dedication.

So at long last here it is... a book for seasoned enthusiasts as well as the "new generation" of Pepsi collector. We hope you enjoy it as much as we have.

Have a Pepsi Day!

Jan Lloyd
Bob Lloyd
Hillsborough, North Carolina

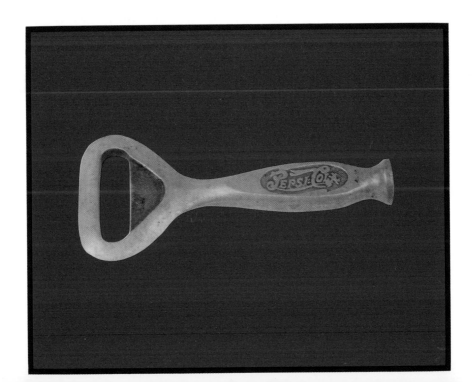

Foreword

During the late nineteenth century, Caleb Davis Bradham was a pharmacist working in his own drug store in New Bern, North Carolina. A young man (in his twenties), Bradham took great pride in working at his soda fountain and in mixing different drinks for his friends. Late in the 1890s, he mixed a drink that was especially satisfying to the townspeople. They began calling the concoction "Brad's Drink." Bradham named his drink Pepsi Cola.

Pharmacist and Pepsi-inventor Caleb Davis Bradham's 1925 renewal license.

For the next few years, Pepsi Cola was sold only at Bradham's soda fountain. Then in July 1902, the pharmacist began advertising Pepsi in the local newspaper. These early ads read: *"Pepsi Cola, 'The Pepsin Drink.' The most refreshing and invigorating drink at soda fountains. Cures headache and improves the appetite. Try it 'for your stomach's sake'— 5 Bradham's Fountain."*

Caleb Bradham, inventor of Pepsi, outside his pharmacy in New Bern, North Carolina.

Bradham began selling Pepsi syrup to other soda fountains, and on December 20, 1902, in New Bern, North Carolina, he formed the first Pepsi Cola Company. Around this time, Bayard Wooted, a woman photographer, helped Bradham to design the famous script trademark of Pepsi Cola. This trademark appeared for the first time in an advertisement in a February 25, 1903, newspaper. (The ad read: "Pepsi Cola, at soda fountains. Exhilarating, invigorating, aids digestion.") Bradham registered the Pepsi Cola trademark with the United States Patent Office on

June 16, 1903.

From 1902 to 1904, sales of the syrup base for Pepsi were exclusively to soda fountains. Then in 1904, Bradham opened a bottling plant in New Bern. The first franchise-bottler to incorporate with the Pepsi Cola name was Henry Fowler of Charlotte, North Carolina, in 1905, and in the same year, Marvin Burnett of Durham began to bottle the drink. To improve sales, Burnett would sneak bottles of the new drink into cases of grape and root beer. Some of his customers returned them, but soon Pepsi Cola caught on. By 1910, there were 280 plants bottling Pepsi Cola.

Pepsi came in six-, six-and-one-half-, and seven-ounce bottles, and by 1910 amber, clear, and aqua glass were all in use. (The most sought-after bottle today is the Hutchinson bottle, distributed only by the Pensacola, Florida, plant.)

Bradham handled all the early advertising for Pepsi. In 1903 or 1904, he issued the first tray, a round six-inch item that bore the trademark in script and presented Pepsi Cola as the "Pepsin Drink." Pictures of attractive women were a mainstay of Bradham's advertising efforts: In 1907, he used the image of a woman from an oil painting (which now hangs in the New Bern Pepsi-Cola plant) on a sign. Perhaps one of the most well known icons of Pepsi Cola advertising

Pepsi-Cola home office in New Bern, North Carolina.

A 1908 photograph of the home office of Pepsi Cola, New Bern, North Carolina.

A framed photograph of Mary Bradham, Caleb Bradham's daughter, drinking a Pepsi.

Oil painting of Mary Bradham. Bradham had considered using this image for advertising purposes but did not. It's the only one of its kind known to be in existence.

Green, and the First Lady of Pepsi—although she was actually the fourth or fifth girl used to sell the drink. Her image appeared on the reproduction tray issued in 1973.

Caleb Bradham remained in control of the Pepsi Cola Company until the early nineteen-twenties. At that time, he made a business mistake, buying sugar heavily at inflated prices just before the bottom fell out of the market. In May of 1923, the Pepsi Cola Company was in bankruptcy, and Davis Caleb Bradham was back where he started at the New Bern pharmacy.

For the next eight years the new owners of the company struggled, and again in 1931 Pepsi went into bankruptcy. Only the Charlotte and Durham Pepsi Cola bottlers were selling Pepsi; the Pepsi company itself was out of business. In 1932, under the direction of its fifth owners, the Pepsi company introduced a twelve-ounce bottle of the drink that sold for 10¢. It took about six months for this size and price to sell well, but by the end of June 1934 the door had once again opened for Pepsi Cola.

was introduced by the New York ad agency that Bradham hired in 1909. With her plumed hat and ruffled sleeves, the model was straight out of the gay nineties. She has been called the Gibson Girl, the Victorian Girl, the Drug-store Girl, the Girl Dressed in

An early-twentieth-century photograph of a drug store with a Gibson-Girl Pepsi-Cola ad on the back wall.

Film star Joan Crawford at Pepsi celebration lends a hand "opening" a giant bottle of Pepsi.

By 1939, three to four hundred bottlers were using a twelve-ounce bottle with a paper label; later they used a printed label with "Pepsi Cola" in block letters. In 1958, the new swirl-style bottle appeared, one that is still being used today in many sizes.

Few advertising items were produced for Pepsi during the nineteen-twenties and thirties. In 1940—the first year that a Pepsi-Cola jingle was heard on the radio—a calendar was issued, and one was produced for every year thereafter. In the late thirties and forties, Pepsi began to advertise with many give-away items bearing their trademark. Today, the headquarters for this product with world-wide distribution are in

An original watercolor from the 1930s of the Pepsi-Cola Company's Laboratories and Headquarters in Long Island City, New York.

Purchase, New York.

Key Dates
28 August 1898: Date of earliest Pepsi-Cola use, as shown from a North Carolina registration.
1902: Pharmacist and Pepsi-Cola inventor Caleb Davis

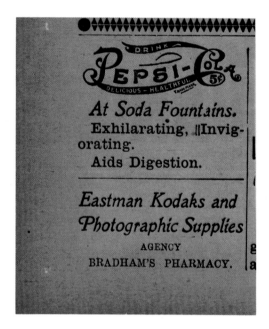

A newspaper clipping advertising Pepsi at Bradham's Pharmacy.

Bradham devotes himself full-time to developing Pepsi Cola.
16 June 1903: Application accepted and Pepsi Cola is registered with the US Patent Office.
20 December 1902: The first Pepsi Cola Company is founded.
25 February 1903: The first advertising using Pepsi Cola's trademark appears. First-year cost for

Newspaper advertisements for Pepsi dated 1903-1907.

advertising is $1,888.78.

1904: Late in the year Pepsi is bottled in the first plant, located in New Bern, North Carolina

1907: Forty bottling plants are in existence.

20 January 1910: First Pepsi-Cola-bottlers convention is held; eighty-seven bottlers from twenty-four states attend.

1932: Pepsi makes its first appearance in twelve-ounce bottles. At first the bottles sell for 10 each; in 1933, the price is dropped to 5.

1939: Three-hundred-and-forty-one bottlers put out a twelve-ounce bottle with a paper label.

1958: The Pepsi "swirl" bottle makes its first appearance.

Early slogans used in Pepsi-Cola Advertising

A refreshing and invigorating beverage

Quiets the nerves

Aids digestion

Tones the system

Guaranteed pure and healthful

Refreshes—invigorates

Refreshing—invigorating

Cures indigestion

Relieves exhaustion

The Pepsin Drink

Delicious—healthful

Strengthening

Satisfying

"There's a difference"— Ask your doctor

"It makes you" eat better, sleep better, look better, feel better

Not only delicious, but good for the blood, the muscle, good all over, makes the cheeks plump and rosy

The health-enhancing properties of Pepsi are touted in these newspaper ads from the 1900s.

For brain fag and body drag

Pepsi Cola strengthens the body

Cooling and satisfying

Makes the body strong

Delicious, invigorating, sustaining

Adapted from the original notes of Everette Lloyd

Early-twentieth-century newspaper ads for Pepsi.

The first Pepsi-Cola delivery truck.

Early Pepsi-Cola wagon drawn by horses.

Chapter I

Bottles, Cans, & Miniatures

Note: Many of the Pepsi bottles included in this chapter have painted lettering. The paint is not original, but was added to make the lettering more visible.

A rare 1905-1910 Hutchinson bottle from the Pensacola, Florida bottling plant.

Amethyst glass with a face on the label. 1908.

A 1908 straight-sided bottle with glass bubbles. The Pepsi logo on the base and shoulder is painted.

A light aqua bottle from 1908.

An amethyst bottle from 1909.

1910 Pepsi bottle from Durham, North Carolina.

The word "Pepsi" is quite pronounced on this 1910 High Point, North Carolina bottle.

A green straight-sided bottle form 1910 with painted Pepsi logos.

This 1910 Durham, North Carolina bottle has a long neck and rounded base.

A circa-1910 aqua bottle from New Bern, North Carolina.

This 1910 bottle has the Pepsi name in block letters on the shoulders and in script at the base.

Opposite page:
Top left: A circa-1910 amber bottle with high shoulders.

Bottom left: An amber bottle from the Ronceverte, West Virginia bottling plant.

Top right: From Goldsboro, North Carolina, a 1907-1912 amber bottle with high shoulders.

Bottom right: A low-shouldered amber bottle with painted logo at the base.

Two amber bottles with low, sloping shoulders and the Pepsi logo painted at the base. Circa 1910.

A light green bottle from the 1910s, with "Pepsi" in large capital letters on the shoulder.

A light aqua bottle with Pepsi painted on the shoulder and base. 1912.

A 1912 Pepsi bottle in blue glass, with straight sides.

Blue-glass bottle with raised lettering; Pepsi log painted at the bottom.

This Pepsi bottle came from a bottling company in High Point, North Carolina. 1920.

A green bottle with the Pepsi-Cola logo painted in six horizontal rows. Circa 1920.

Embossed Pepsi bottle with painted logo; circa 1925.

A 1927 green-glass bottle form Richmond, Virginia, with the name running vertically.

Scalloped glass on a Pepsi bottle from New Bern, North Carolina; circa 1928.

A small bottle with a short neck. 1928.

A small bottle with "draped" glass. From 1928.

A clear bottle form 1928, with decorative bands of roughed glass around the neck and shoulders.

Three narrow-waisted bottles in green glass. 1931.

A bright green bottle with a long neck and sloping shoulder from the 1930s. The neck and shoulders have a band of roughed glass.

the 1930s.

Pepsi bottle with label in Spanish. 1940s.

One-quart bottle with label. 1940s.

This Evervess club soda bottle (manufactured bt the Pepsi-Cola Company) from the 1940s has a paper label.

Pepsi bottle with label in French. 1950s.

Paper bottle labels from the 1940s.

A twenty-inch glass display
bottle from the 1960s.

A group of Pepsi bottle caps. The different colors indicate
which town or time a bottle came from.

A circa-1940 cone-top can

A cone-top can from the 1940s.

Cone-top can from the 1940s.

Two six-packs of miniature Pepsi bottles. From the 1950s.

A seven-ounce can from the 1970s.

Miniature bottles with paper labels.

Chapter II

Bottle Openers & Stoppers

A 1940s brass bottle opener.

Starr X brand stationary bottle openers and box.

Bottle openers in various shapes.

Bottle stoppers with the Pepsi logo.

Chapter III

Racks, Carriers, & Cartons

A 1930s bottle rack with die-cut Pepsi bottles on each end.

A carton display stand from the 1930s.

A bag rack from the 1930s.

A paper carrier with a woven-basket print. Circa 1940.

A paper carrier bag from the 1930s.

Two 1930s six-pack carriers for "BIG" twelve-ounce bottles.

A cardboard six-pack carrier from the 1940s.

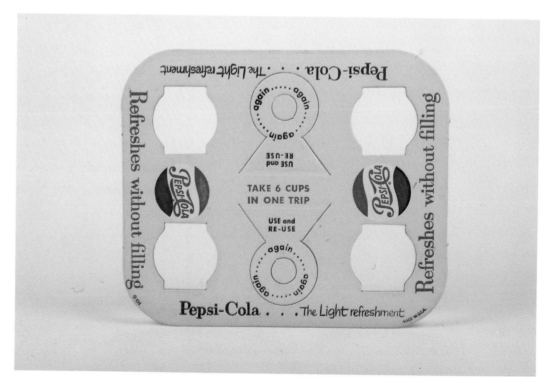

An unfolded six-pack cardboard carrier from the 1950s.

This cardboard carrier from the 1950s holds four sixteen-ounce bottles.

A 1960s six-pack carrier.

A wood railroad crate used to transport 5-cent bottles of Pepsi.

An early wooden carrier with some damage to the sides.

A 1930s wooden carrying case with a red Pepsi bottle on the side.

Wooden box with hand openings on the short sides. From the 1940s.

A wooden 1930s Pepsi bottle carrier with pull-up handle.

From the 1940s, a wooden "Handy Home" carrier.

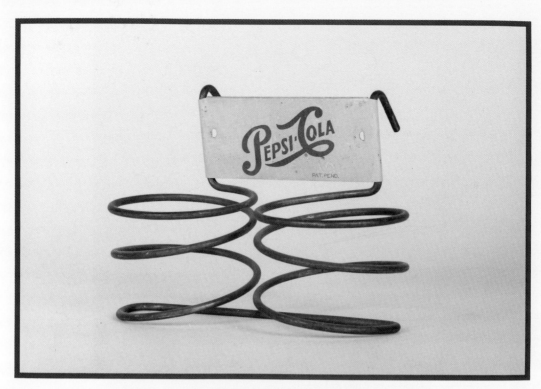

A two-bottle holder, circa 1950.

A 1950s "retoter" to carry two bottles.

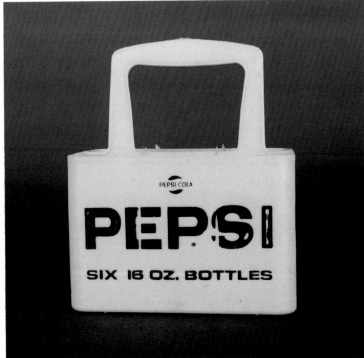

This 1960s yellow plastic bottle carrier holds six sixteen-ounce bottles.

An aluminum bottle carrier from the 1930s with the double-dot Pepsi logo.

A 1950s aluminum bottle carrier.

Chapter IV

Trays

A 1905 six-inch tip tray.

This 1905 tip tray has a distinctive border.

A rare horizontal tip
tray from 1906.

REFRESHING

DRINK

Pepsi=Cola

DELICIOUS · HEALTHFUL   5¢

INVIGORATING

A 1908 tip tray.

A serving tray from 1908.

Opposite page:
Top left: Tip tray from 1909 with the Gibson Girl image.

Top right: A 1909 serving tray featuring the Gibson Girl.

Bottom left: A tip from 1910.

Bottom right: A 1910 serving tray.

A 1939 serving tray with a bottle of Pepsi laid diagonally across a map of the United States.

A late 1930s serving tray advertising Pepsi bottled by the J. F. Giering Company.

A serving tray from the 1940s showing three children reading a music book. With the slogan "Pepsi Cola Hits the Spot, Twelve Full Ounces, That's Alot."

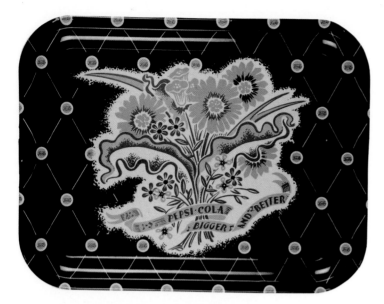

This colorful serving tray is from 1940.

Serving tray from the 1940s.

A 1940s serving tray.

A 1950s serving tray advertising Everess Sparkling Water, a Pepsi product.

This lively Coney-Island beach scene makes for a colorful serving tray. Most of the beachgoers—including some of the swimmers—are drinking bottles of Pepsi. 1950s.

Square serving tray from the 1950s.

Pepsi flows from a just-opened bottle on this 1960s serving tray.

A serving tray from the 1960s.

Ice appears to cover the surface of this serving tray from the 1970s.

A Spanish tip tray from the 1970s.

Opposite page:
A rare 1909 four-sided tin straw holder featuring the Gibson
Girl in a soda parlor.

Chapter V

Fountain Items

A tin straw holder from the 1930s.

From the 1930s, a stoneware straw holder.

1930s straw box with straw.

A stoneware spoon holder from the 1930s.

A 1930s-1940s metal napkin dispenser.

The straws (with Pepsi logo) are visible through the clear
section of this 1950s straw box.

Two soda-fountain Pepsi glasses from the 1940s with syrup fill lines.

Three Wellsville china plates with the logo of Pepsi-Cola and two other Pepsi products, Orange Crush and NuGrape, on the rims.

Two tapered fountain cup holders from the 1940s.

A fountainhead in the shape of a Pepsi bottle.

A plastic pour spout with a cork end that fits into a bottle. Circa 1940.

Ceramic Pepsi dispenser, circa 1900. This rare and gorgeous piece is decorated with rabbits and trees with brass foliage. The lid says that Pepsi "Cures indigestion, relieves exhaustion."

A circa-1920 milk-glass dispenser. The syrup jug on top is from the 1950s.

A musical tap knob with the Pepsi bottle cap logo on the top. Made by Tap-Rite products Corporation, Hackensack, New Jersey.

A soda dispenser from the 1950s. Stainless steel, made by the Multiplex Faucet Company, St. Louis, Missouri.

Large seltzer bottles from the early twentieth century.

A chrome-over-brass painted sign form a drugstore-counter dispenser.

A 1910-1915 Pepsi syrup jug, one-gallon size.

Two clear-glass syrup bottles from 1943 with applied colored labels. The sides are embossed with the Pepsi logo in vertical bands.

This green wooden syrup barrel with iron bands has a Pepsi ad on the lid.

A drum motif adorns this concentrate container from the 1930s.

A concentrate container from the 1940s.

A bright red concentrate drum with the "A Nickel's Drink—Worth a Dime" slogan around the base.

A 1930s menu board with a chalkboard center.

A one-gallon can of fountain syrup. 1950s.

A circa-1940 syrup can and lid.

A rare wooden board from the 1930s or 1940s. It has slots for menu items and declares the Pepsi "Goes Great with a Sandwich!" ◄◄

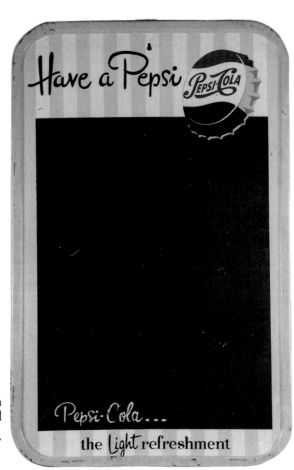

A press-tin menu board with a yellow edge and chalkboard center from the 1950s. ►►

This tin menu board is from the 1940s and lists one of "Today's Specials" as "Pepsi-Cola, 6 for—(plus deposit)." ◄◄

From 1968, this pressed-metal menu board has a chalkboard insert and a bright yellow border. ►►

A rubber change mat from the 1970s.

A brown plastic menu board from the 1970s.

A Pepsi menu board with a chalkboard center,
from 1975.

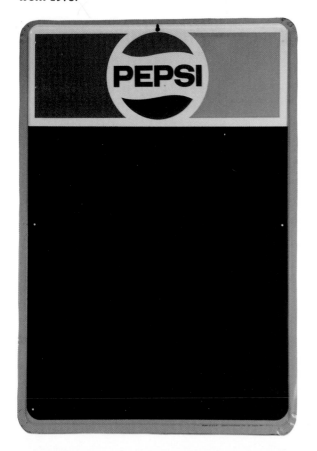

An oval change mat.

Change receiver from the 1970s.

Pepsi and Pete, the Pepsi-Cola cops, on an apron from the 1930s.

A soda-jerk cap from the 1930s.

Paper vendor's cap from the 1960s.

CHAPTER VI

Sales & Promotional Items

A table to help bottlers calculate profit. 1950s.

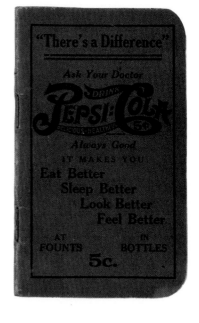

A red memo book from 1914 touting the health value of Pepsi.

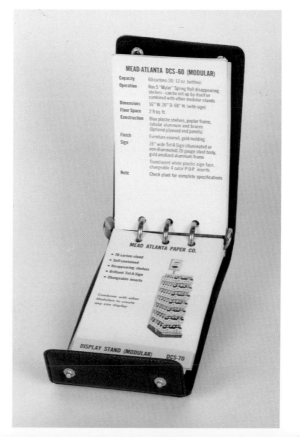

From the 1950s, a salesman's loose-leaf Pepsi merchandise book.

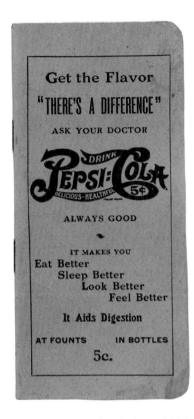

A yellow memo book from 1914.

From the 1920s, two small memo pads with grid paper. On the front cover is the slogan "I Love Its Flavor" and on the back is: "Discriminating People who Desire Refreshment, Health, Mental Alertness, Pep, and Vitality Drink Pepsi."

Two sides of a 1940 cardboard fan featuring the Pepsi-Cola cops.

From 1938, a 38th anniversary illustrated bottler's book.

Two sides of a 1912 cardboard fan. A calendar is on the back.

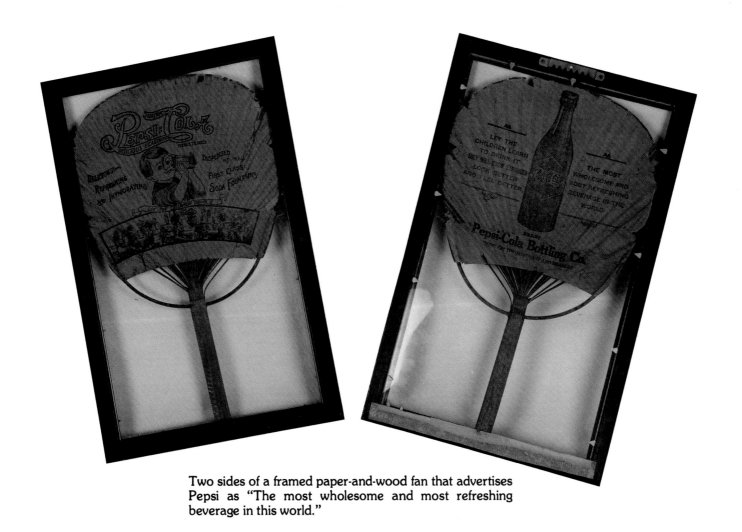

Two sides of a framed paper-and-wood fan that advertises Pepsi as "The most wholesome and most refreshing beverage in this world."

A 1940s Pepsi bottle-cap pin back.   Four ad pins from the 1940s and 1950s.

A bottle topper from the 1930s, with bottle.

Pepsi-Cola bottle-cap pinback.

An example of the records that Pepsi produced during World War II, on which service men could place messages to friends and family back in the U.S.

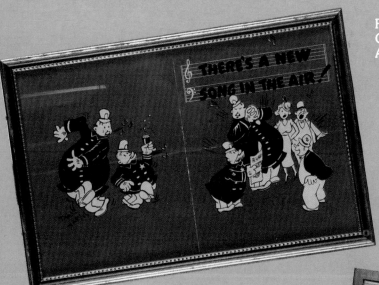

Framed sheet music, front and back, of the 1940s "Pepsi-Cola Radio Jingle," written by Auten Croom-Johnson and Alan Kent.

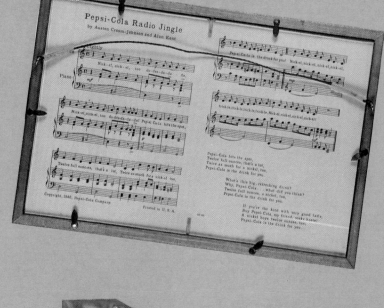

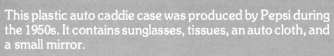

This plastic auto caddie case was produced by Pepsi during the 1950s. It contains sunglasses, tissues, an auto cloth, and a small mirror.

Pepsi-Cola coaster.

A four-piece coaster set from the 1970s. The gold-tone coasters are a wagon-wheel shape with an enamel Pepsi logo in the center.

A large Pepsi display bottle from the 1970s.

Opposite page:
A hard-to-find calendar from 1909, with the Gibson Girl and the slogan "Pepsi-Cola Feeds The Nerves."

Chapter VII

Calendars

A 1911 framed calendar with a girl sipping Pepsi through a straw.

A 1921 calendar with a Rolf Armstrong illustration of "The Pepsi-Cola Girl."

A very rare 1913 calendar showing the July page. The slogan reads "Drink Pepsi-Cola for Brain Fag and Body Drag."

A 1941 calendar from the Pepsi-Cola Bottling Company of Plymouth, Massachusetts.

A painting by Dale Nichols of a snow-covered farm illustrates this first pate of a 1942 Pepsi calendar.

The story of the Pepsi-Cola calendar is clipped onto the front of this example from 1945, illustrated with the winning painting from the Pepsi-Cola Competition for American Artists.

A 1946 Pepsi calendar.

A Pepsi calendar from 1947.

Pepsi's Annual Art Competition and Exhibition produced
this illustration for the first month of the 1949 calendar.

An ice skater in a vibrant blue-and-white outfit highlights this page of the 1950 Pepsi calendar.

A metal calendar with the day of the week, date, and month on rotating wheels.

A cardboard frame surrounds this 1954 calendar.

A plastic calendar from 1968.

The logo for Diet Pepsi appears in one corner of this 1965 "Presidents of the United States" Pepsi calendar.

A 1982 classroom calendar with the Pepsi logo in the background.

CHAPTER VIII

Cardboard Signs

Matted and framed, this 15¾" x 24" poster is the only one of its size known to exist. Dating from 1907, it is printed on heavy cardboard and bears the slogan: "Drink Pepsi-Cola, 'The American Beverage.'"

From 1905, a "Miss Pepsi-Cola" poster with faux gold frame.

A 1909 poster

A heavy cardboard sign.

An extremely rare poster of a girl seated at a glass-topped soda table with a bottle and glass of Pepsi. Circa 1910-1915.

A heavy cardboard poster from around 1910. The girl shown is holding a bottle with a straw.

A circa-1919 poster of Rolf Armstrong's Pepsi-Cola Girl. it measures 22" x 28" and is pictured here in the original Pepsi-Cola frame.

A cardboard sign from the 1920s has a floral border and simply says "Pepsi-Cola."

A cardboard sign advertising the twelve-ounce bottle of Pepsi.

A 1930s cardboard sign.

A cardboard sign with the slogan: "A Nickels Drink—Worth A Dime."

A late 1930s or early 1940s poster of a girl at the beach with her cooler of drinks and a Pepsi bottle cap in the sky.

Musical notes dance around the slogan "Sing out for Pepsi!" on this 1940s circular cardboard sign.

From the 1940s, a poster with a gardener in red overalls advertising the twelve-ounce Pepsi bottle.

A 25" x 34" self-framed cardboard sign illustrated with a woman in a backless dress.

This framed cardboard sign of a girl in an apple tree is from the 1940s. The Pepsi bottle has two straws.

From the 1940s, a self-framed cardboard sign. The illustration of a girl with ice skates and a bottle of Pepsi is by Mozert.

An oval Pepsi-Cola logo adorns this self-framed cardboard sign from the 1940s.

Signed by the artist, Ann Rose, this self-framed cardboard sign from the 1940s features a young woman dressed in patriotic stars-and stripes.

A woman in a white one-piece bathing suit holds a bottle of Pepsi while a sail boat travels past in the water behind her. A 1940s self-framed cardboard signed by J. Erbit.

Price Guide: Pepsi-Cola Collectibles

Values vary immensely according to the condition of the piece, the location of the market, and the overall quality of the design and manufacture. Condition is always of paramount importance in assigning a value. Prices vary by geographic location and those at specialty antique shows will vary from those at general shows. And, of course, being in the right place at the right time may make all the difference.

All these factors make it impossible to create an absolutely accurate reference, but we can offer a guide. To use this guide well it is necessary to know that the left hand number is the **page** number. The letters following it indicate the **position** of the photograph on the page: T=top, L=left, TL=top left, TC=top center, TR=top right, C=center, CL=center left, CR=center right, R=right, B=bottom, BL=bottom left, BC=bottom center, BR=bottom right. The italicized single digit represents the **location** of the piece in a photograph with more than one object from left to right and top row first and bottom row second when there is more than one row beginning with the number *1*. The last numbers are the estimated **value** ranges in U.S. dollars.

page	position	location	dollar value
9	BL		90-110
	BR		55-65
10	TR		55-65
	BL		55-65
12	C		315-385
13	TL		95-115
	BC		60-70
14	TL		90-110
15	BL		60-70
	C		60-70
	TR		60-70
16	TL		60-70
	BR		120-150
17	TL		120-150
	BL		450-550
	TR		550-650
	BR		170-210
18	TL		40-50
	BC		40-50
	TR		40-50
19	TR		395-485
20	TL		90-110
	C		225-275
	BR		60-70
21	C		60-70
	TR		35-45
22	TL		45-55 ea.
	C		35-45
23			60-70
24	BC		35-45
25	CL		5-10
	TR		10-20
	BR		25-35
26	TL		40-50
	C		40-50
	BR		40-50
27	CL		5-10
	TR		45-55 ea.
28	CL		75-90
	BC		15-20
29	TC	2&3	20-25
	TC	4	45-55
	TC	5	30-40
30	CL		900-1300
	BR		150-180
31	TC		270-330
	BL		30-40
32	TL		15-25 ea.
	BC		35-45
	TR		55-65
33	TL		20-30
	BR		20-30
34	TL		90-110
	CR		90-110
	CL		90-110
	BR		90-110
35	TL		65-75
	BR		65-75
36	TC		30-40
	BC		25-55
37	TL		25-35
	TR		5-10
	BR		20-30
38	CL		2700-3300
	BR		1620-1980
39	T		2250-2750
	BL		1600-2000
	BR		1385-1695
40	TL		1080-1320
	TR		695-850
41	TR		180-220
	CL		330-400
	BR		45-55
42	TL		40-50
	TR		50-60
	CL		45-55
	BL		25-35
	BR		25-35
43	TL		35-45
	CL		30-40
	BR		30-40
44			25-35
45			5400-6600
46	TL		225-275
	TC		445-545
	BR		150-180
47	TR		375-455
	BR		200-250
48	TR	1	35-45
	TR	2	20-30
	CL		360-440
49	T		100-130 ea.
	BL		90-110
	BR		20-30
50	TL		9000-11000
	TR		45-55
	BR		315-385
51	TL		180-220
	TR		340-420
52	TL		270-330
	CR		20-30 ea.
	BL		270-330
53	TL		450-550
	TR		450-550
	BL		450-550
54	TL		45-55
	TR		85-105
	BL		40-50
55	TL		160-195
	TR		55-65
	BL		135-165
	BR		20-30
56	TL		5-10
	TR		10-20
	BL		10-20
	BR		10-20
57	TL		10-20
	TR		135-165
	BL		35-45
	BR		25-35
58	CR		45-55
59	TL		45-55
	TR		45-55 ea.
	B		25-35
60	T		45-55
	B		1500 (complete)
61	T		180-220
	BL		10-20
	BR		35-45 set
62	TL		10-20
	TR		70-90
	CL/BC		50-60
63	T		55-65
	B		20-30
64	TL		20-30
	BL		20-30
65			2700-3300
66	TL		3150-3850
	CR		1800-2200
	BL		720-880
67	TR		270-330
	CL		45-55
	BR		30-40
68	TL		25-35
	CR		35-45
	BL		35-45
69	TL		160-195
	CR		10-20
	BL		15-25
70	CL		15-25
	BR		5-15
71			9000-11000
72	TL		2250-2750
	CR		2250-2750
	BL		1800-2200
73	TR		1620-1980
	CL		1080-1320
	BR		1980-2420
74	TC		315-385
	CL		150-180
	CR		55-65
75	T		315-385
	BL		315-385
	BR		180-220

No.	Pos		Value
76			810-990
77	TL		270-330
	CR		70-90
	BL		450-550
78	TL		495-605
	BR		540-660
79	T		180-220
	BL		315-385
	BR		450-550
80	TL		45-55
	CL		135-165
	BR		80-100
81	TR		55-65
	CR		65-85
	BL		180-220
82	TL		60-70
	BL		45-55
	BR		3600-4400
83	TL		3600-4400
	TR		90-110
	CR		540-660
	BL		315-385
84	TL		15-25
	CL		160-195
	CR		90-110
	BL		90-110
86	TL		35-45
	BR		45-55
87	TL		35-45
	BR		55-65
89	TL		35-45
90	CL		180-220
	BR		90-110
91	TL		65-75
	BR		40-50
92	TL		35-45
	CR		35-45
93	CL		65-75
	BR		60-70
94	C		1260-1540
	B		1350-1650
95	T		225-275
96			10800-13200
97	TL		1260-1680
	CR		160-195
	BL		540-660
98	TL		1260-1680
99	TL		450-550

No.	Pos		Value
	CR		270-330
	BL		225-275
100	T		135-165
	CL		110-135
	BC		70-80
101	TL		225-275
	BL		495-605 pair
102	L		360-440
	R		250-300
103	TL		225-275
	BL		165-205
104	TL		125-155
	TR		115-145
	BL		360-440
107			45-55
108	TL		35-45
110	BR		85-105
111	C		120-150
	BR		330-405
112	TL		125-155
	BL		45-55
	BR		35-45
113	L		25-35
	TR		50-60
	BR		15-25
114	CR		15-25
115		*1*	675-825
		2	450-550
116	TL		1200-1500
	TR		110-130
117	T		250-300
	B		10-20
118	TL		85-105
119			180-220
120	T		75-100
	BL		25-35
121	CL		470-575
	BR		270-330
122			250-275
123	TL		75-95
	BR		440-550
124	BL		10-20
125	C		225-275
	B		225-275
126	TR		225-275
	CL		70-90
	BR		95-115
128	TL		790-970
130	CL		10-20

No.	Pos		Value
131	T		10-20 ea.
	BL		90-110
	BR		55-65
132			15-25
133	TL		20-30
	BL		45-55
	BR		20-30
134	TR		3-5 ea.
	BL		10-20
137	B	3	55-65
138	CL		110-130 ea.
	BR		25-35
139	TL		35-45
	CR		55-65
	BR	*2*	5-15
140	BL		135-165
142			35-45
143	T		45-65
	B		135-165
145			540-660
146	TL		90-110
	CL/BR		45-55
147			95-115
148	TL		360-440
	TR		275-325
	CL/BC		110-130
149	TL		25-35
	TR		60-70
	BR		40-50 with box
150	CR		30-40
	BL		5-15
151	TR		25-35
	BR		5-15 ea.
152	TL		15-25
	CL		10-20
	BR		100-120
153	T		10-20
	CL		10-20
	BR		5-15
154	BR		30-40
155	B	*1*	25-35
157	BR		115-165
158	CL		65-80
159	TL		45-55
	BL		45-55
	R		65-80
160	TL		65-80 ea.
	CL		5-10
	BL		65-80

A 1940s cardboard poster featuring a photograph of a girl surrounded by yellow roses. On her raised glass is the slogan: "Pepsi Cola Hits the Spot."

From the 1940s, an 18" x 23" cardboard sign of a girl in a bonnet tied with a veil. She holds a bottle of "Sparkling" Pepsi.

A 1940s Erbit illustration of a young woman at the beach. Cardboard.

Pepsi bottle caps fly over a golden horizon on this 1940s cardboard sign.

A cowgirl in a brightly colored shirt advertises the "Big Big Bottle" of Pepsi in this 1940s cardboard sign.

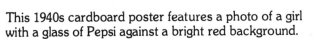

This 1940s cardboard poster features a photo of a girl with a glass of Pepsi against a bright red background.

From the 1950s, a cardboard sign with an illustration of a slender young woman in black-and-purple striped pants advertises that Pepsi "Refreshes without filling."

A picnic scene from the 1950s advertises Pepsi as "The Light Refreshment." Self-framed cardboard.

An 18" x 26" cardboard poster featuring a couple enjoying Pepsi at the lakeside.

A large cardboard sign with the "More Bounce to the Ounce" logo. 1950s.

An easel-back vertical cardboard sign.

A little girl stands on a crate of Pepsi bottles in order to open the child-size bottle next to her in this rare framed cardboard window display.

A 1930s die-cut Pepsi-Cola cop running with a Pepsi sign.

Pepsi and Pete, The Pepsi-Cola cops, scratch an advertisement in the sand at the feet of a girl at the beach. 1930s die-cut cardboard counter piece with easel back.

Two die-cut 1930s cops advertise a "Bigger Better" carton of Pepsi.

A late 1930s or early 1940s die-cut cardboard sign with easel back.

A ten-inch tall die-cut cardboard bottle that contains a recipe booklet. Mid-1940s.

An easel-back cardboard bottle.

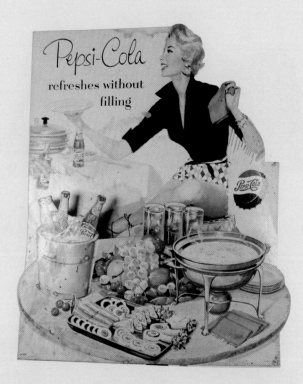

This 3-D cardboard sign from the 1950s shows a picnic scene.

Signed by Bawler, this 1950s cardboard sign features a three-dimensional tennis player.

A framed die-cut cardboard sign, circa 1940.

This twenty-inch cardboard Santa sign is from the 1950s and features a "Season's Greetings" bottle cap.

From the 1960s, a cardboard display sign with Santa Claus holding a bottle of Pepsi. Approximately 20".

A 1960s dancing Santa drawn by Norman Rockwell. About 20".

Nearly two-feet tall, this 1960s Santa is wearing buckle boots and is standing in front of a ranch-style house with a Christmas tree in its front window.

A cardboard sign with an Easter motif: a chick breaking out of an egg that contains a small bottle of Pepsi. From the late 1960s or early 1970s.

The front of a two-sided sign welcoming Pepsi bottlers to a convention.

On the back of the sign, a worker positions the rabbit above the brim of the hat.

Opposite page:
A self-standing Norman Rockwell Santa. 60" tall.

Chapter IX

Celluloid Signs

A 1940s nine-inch diameter celluloid sign.

A celluloid sign from the 1940s.

A late-1940s or early-1950s celluloid sign.

A circa-1950 bottle cap celluloid sign.

A young woman talks on the phone while holding a bottle of Pepsi on this oval celluloid sign from the 1950s.

The two metal knobs at the bottom of this 1950s oval celluloid sign were meant to hold a calendar.

This celluloid sign from the 1960s advertises Pepsi in Spanish.

A small yellow rectangular sign with the "Say 'Pepsi, Please'" slogan.

A celluloid sign from 1960 featuring an African-American couple.

The "You've got a lot to live! Pepsi's got a lot to give!" slogan on a celluloid sign from the 1960s.

Chapter X

Metal Signs

From the early 1900s, a tin sign with raised lettering.

A yellow border surrounds this rare tin sign that advertises
a five-cent bottle of Pepsi. Early 1900s.

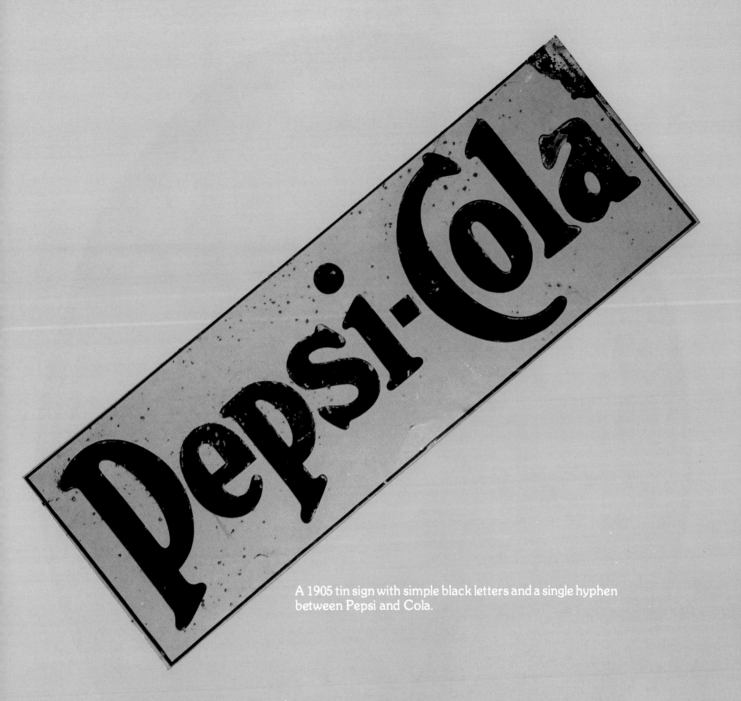

A 1905 tin sign with simple black letters and a single hyphen between Pepsi and Cola.

A small tin sign from 1905-1910.

A rare 1908 oval tin sign. 8 ½" x 10 ½".

A halo seems to surround the narrow-waisted bottle on this 1910-1915 framed tin sign.

A 1910-1915 tin sign with a dark green border and red background.

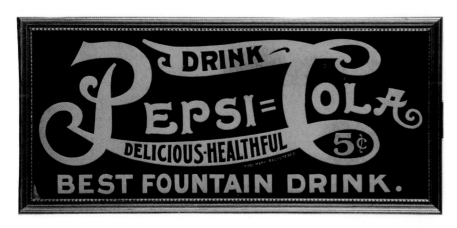

A back-bar sign from the early 1900s.

A tin sign from the 1930s shows a six-pack of "Refreshing and Healthful" Pepsi.

A 1930s sidewalk sign made of textured pressed aluminum. It calls Pepsi "America's biggest nickel's worth."

This 1930s bag rack has a tin sign illustrated with two Pepsi-Cola cops.

Possibly from Canada, this blue and yellow tin sign was produced after the introduction of the twelve-ounce bottle in the early 1930s.

An embossed tin sign from the 1930s.

From the 1930s, a blue-edged tin sign with the slogan "America's Biggest Nickel's Worth."

A tin sign advertising five-cent bottles of Pepsi. 1930s.

This very narrow 1930s tin sign features four Pepsi-Cola cops.

This tin sign advertises ice-cold Pepsi with red and white lettering on a green background.

A two-sided tin sign from the 1930s.

A large 1930s tin sign framed by a raised border.

From the late 1930s or early 1940s, a tin sign in the shape of a twelve-ounce bottle of Pepsi.

A tin sign from the 1930s, with a "Look for the Trademark" arrow above the bottle's label.

This tin bottle from the 1940s is forty inches tall.

This bottle-shaped tin sign from the 1940s is thirty inches tall.

Pepsi promises "More Bounce to the Ounce" on this late-1940s embossed tin sign.

"Please count your change and don't forget the Pepsi-Cola" is the reminder printed on this 1940s cash register sign.

A vertical enameled-porcelain sign from the 1940s. The Pepsi bottle appears to be bursting through a paper background.

A door plate from the 1940s.

A door handle with the Pepsi-Cola logo and slogan. From the 1940s.

A string holder from the 1940s.

This large bottle cap with a red, white, and blue ribbon
behind it illustrates a 1950s tin sign.

A 1950s tin sign.

An embossed tin bottle cap, with a three-foot diameter, from the 1960s.

Chapter XI

Miscellaneous Signs & Mirrors

A 1940s masonite sign with pink plastic letters.

Its streamlined logo indicates that this fiberboard sign was used during the 1950s.

From the 1950s, a porcelain sign in yellow with blue and red lettering.

An electric, light-up sign from the 1950s.

A 1960s embossed-plastic sign.

From the 1960s, an embossed-plastic and metal sign. When the sign is running, the glass "fills" with Pepsi.

A plastic sign from the 1970s.

From the 1950s, a Pepsi mirror.

In this 1950s mirror, the woman's face is seen in reflection.

Chapter XII

Thermometers

From the 1930s, this mirrored sign includes a thermometer.

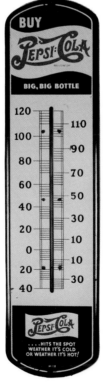

This thermometer from the 1930s says that "Pepsi-Cola hits the spot weather it's cold or weather it's hot!"

The straw is the mercury tube on this 1930s thermometer.

A thermometer from the 1940s advertises Pepsi's twelve-ounce bottle as "Bigger and Better."

A bottle cap decorates the top of this 1940s thermometer.

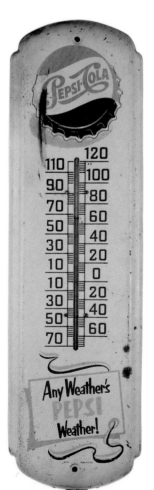

A thermometer from the 1950s.

This 1950s thermometer describes Pepsi as "The Light Refreshment".

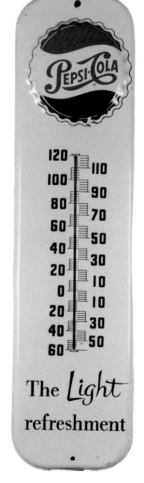

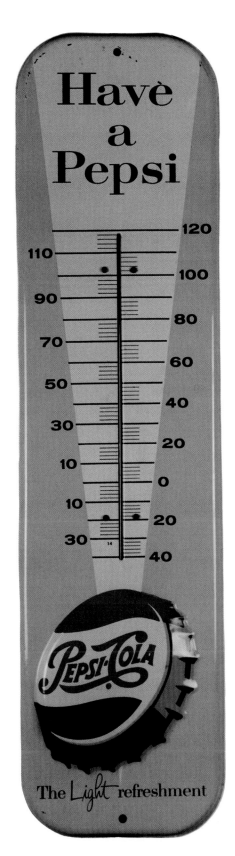

From the Pam Clock Corporation, a 1950s thermometer.

A wedge of white plunges toward lower temperatures and a Pepsi bottle cap on this 1950s thermometer.

A plastic thermometer from the 1960s with a simple Pepsi logo.

A metal thermometer from the 1970s.

The Stout Sign Company of St. Louis, Missouri, made this white thermometer in the 1970s.

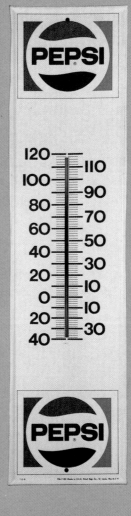

Made by the Skioto Sign Company in Ohio, this thermometer from the 1970s reads "say 'Pepsi, Please.'"

CHAPTER XIII

Clocks

Two 1920s musical clocks from Germany. "Drink Pepsi-Cola" is written on the clock faces; when wound, the ballerinas under each face turn and the clocks play the Pepsi-Cola jingle.

A Pepsi bottle cap is at the center of this plastic-and-metal electric clock from the 1940s.

An example of the earliest neon clocks produced by Pepsi Cola. From the 1930s.

A metal wall clock from the 1940s.

A wood case surrounds this wall clock from the 1940s.

A "can" clock from General Electric.

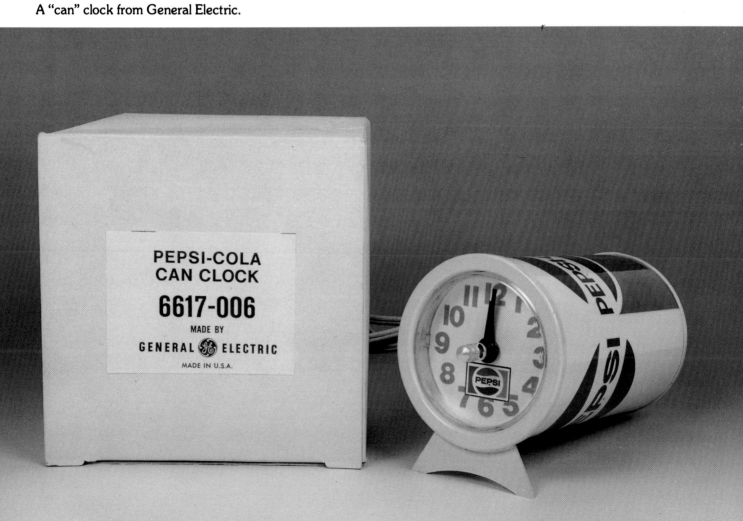

An electric clock from the 1950s.

The bottle cap is behind the hands on this circa-1950 electric clock.

This bottle-cap shaped clock from the 1950s lights up.

A plastic electric clock from the 1950s.

Simplified Pepsi logo on an electric clock from the 1970s.

Chapter XIV

Radios

This Bakelite bottle radio from the 1930s features a "sparkling" Pepsi logo.

A 1940s Pepsi-bottle radio. The plastic top is a dial.

From the 1950s, a radio that looks like a Pepsi bottle. The
top and bottom twist to offer volume and station control.

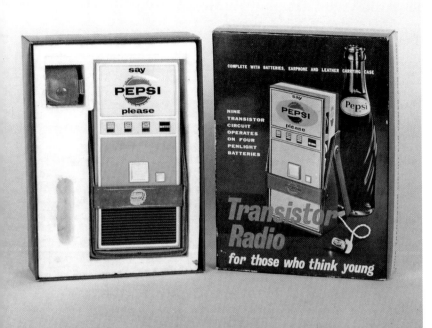

This machine-style radio in its original box is from the 1960s and has a "Say Pepsi Please" logo.

This blue plastic radio from the 1950s is shaped to resemble an ice cooler; the tuning and volume dials on either side look like bottle caps.

A soda machine-style Pepsi radio with a leather carrying case from the 1950s.

A 1967 floor cooler-style plastic radio. The controls are beneath the flip top.

A circa-1964 radio shaped to look like a soda dispenser for a fast-food restaurant. Roughly seven inches tall, it has leather carrying handles.

Two five-inch can-style transistor radios with the speaker on top and the volume and tuning controls (twin wheels) on opposite sides. The yellow box is the original packaging for each radio.

Chapter XV

Ink Blotters

A yellow ink blotter from 1905.

1905 ink blotter.

1905 ink blotter in blue.

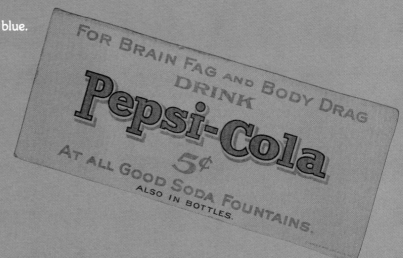

Pepsi and Pete, the Pepsi cops, appear on this 1939 ink blotter.

Ink blotter from the 1940s.

CHAPTER XVI

Coolers

Three views of a wooden ice cooler. The Pepsi logo is on
one section; Orange Crush and Good Grape (distributed
through Pepsi) are advertised on the other sections.

An early Pepsi ice cooler. Metal, with Pepsi ads on all four sides.

An interior view of the 1930s cooler. The inside of the hinged lid reminds customers to "Drink Pepsi-Cola."

A Pepsi ice cooler from the 1930s.

A large blue metal Pepsi ice cooler.

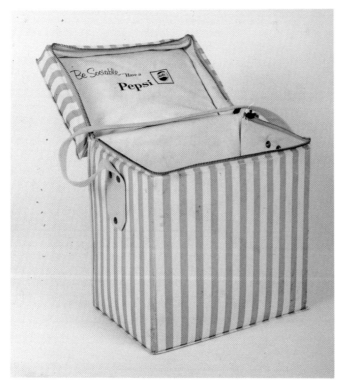

A striped vinyl cooler from the 1950s. The Pepsi logo is on the inside of the lid.

A cylindrical vinyl cooler with a Tiffany's glass motif. 1970s.

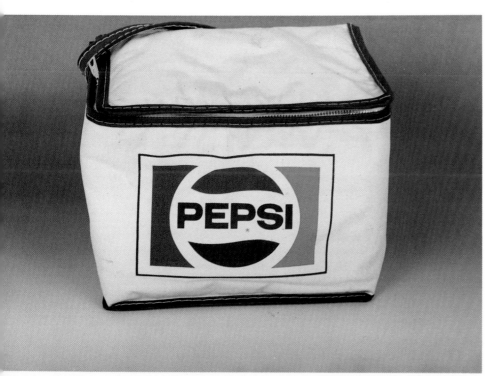

A vinyl cooler from the 1970s.

Chapter XVII

Lighters, Matchbooks, & Ashtrays

A 1940s lucite desk lighter with an embedded bottle cap.

A can lighter from the 1940s.

Bottle-shaped lighters and box from the 1940s and 1950s.
The necks come off to expose the lighter element.

This 1950s musical lighter plays the jingle "Pepsi-Cola Hits
the Spot." The winder is on the back.

A Nesor musical Hi-Fi lighter from the 1950s.

A Crown harp-shaped lighter in gold. 1950s.

This yellow lighter with bottle-cap logo was made in the 1950s by Penguin.

This 1950s lighter was manufactured by Rosen.

A 1950s silver lighter with enameled bottle cap, by Zippo.

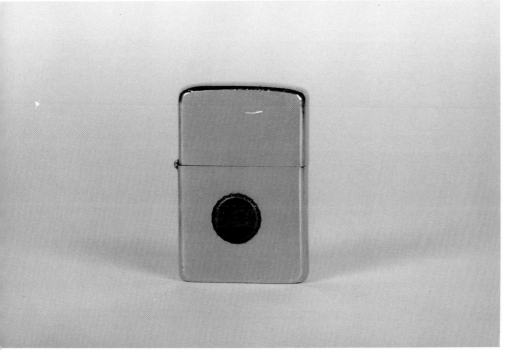

A lighter from the 1960s.

Matchbook covers from the 1930s.

A gold New Bern promotional
lighter from the 1960s.

Seven of twelve matchbooks that came in a 1940s boxed
set. They feature different units of the US Armed
Services—and Disney characters.

A plastic ash tray from the 1960s.

A clear glass ash tray commemorating the opening of a
Pepsi-Cola bottling plant in San Diego, California, 1963.

A metal cigarette holder advertising the Pepsi product
Evervess Sparkling Water.

Chapter XVIII

Desk Accessories & Pens

A Lucite cube with embedded Pepsi bottle cap and "Pepsi Power" star burst.

A silver pen-and-pencil set with the Pepsi logo on the top of each implement. From the 1960s.

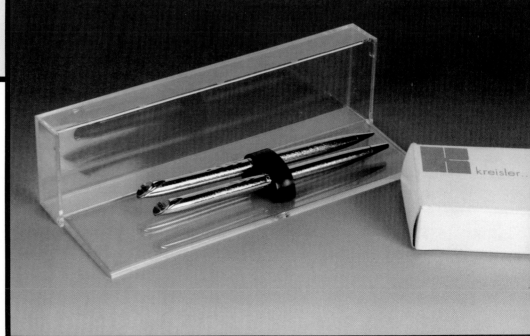

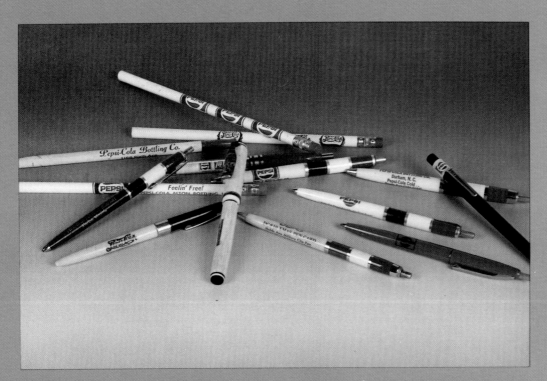

A variety of Pepsi pens and pencils.

A group of pens from the 1930s and 1940s, including one
with a bottle floating in oil in its center.

CHAPTER XIX

Household & Personal Items

Five early watch fobs.

A sewing kit from the 1940s. It reads, "Just Sew You'll Remember."

A 1940s toothpick holder.

Three sets of salt shakers. The center and left sets (with metal tops) are from the 1930s; the set on the right (with plastic lids) is from the 1950s.

Tie bar and key chain from the 1950s.

Fashioned from gold by the late Tom Avery, a noted Pepsi collector, this Pepsi bottle cap necklace was a gift to this author. Only four are in existence.

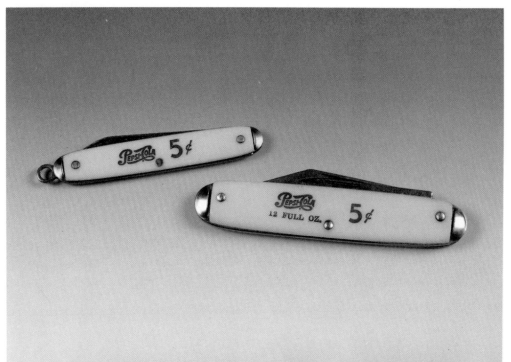

Two pocket knives from the 1950s.

Pepsi key chain, circa 1950.

A blue metal folding chair from the 1950s. It has a striped vinyl seat and a Pepsi slogan on the back rest.

A cloth napkin with "Pepsi Co." embroidered at the edge.

Pepsi-Cola commemorative glasses featuring Warner Brothers characters: From left to right: The Roadrunner; Beaky Buzzard; Tweety; Wile E. Coyote; Sylvester; and Speedy Gonzales.

Top view of a 1950s card table with a Pepsi bottle cap in the center.

A Pepsi candlestick telephone, circa 1970.

This plastic hanging lamp from the 1970s looks like stained glass.

A leaded glass hanging lamp from the 1970s.

A scarf with the Pepsi logo from the 1950s.

A 1960s "Feelin' Free!" cap.

A pattern of bottle caps brightens this 1960s scarf.

Chapter XX

Toys & Games

From the 1930s or 1940s, a wood and masonite Buddy L
delivery truck.

A 1930s composition gull-wing cooler bank.

Opposite page:
This blue plastic miniature vending machine from the 1940s dispenses a mini bottle of Pepsi when a nickel is inserted.

The cover of a cardboard pocket baseball game from the 1930s.

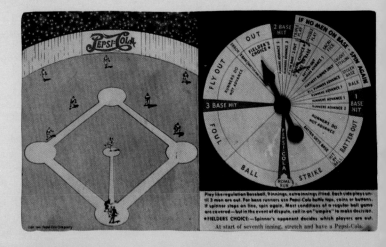

The inside of the pocket baseball game, showing a spinner and playing field.

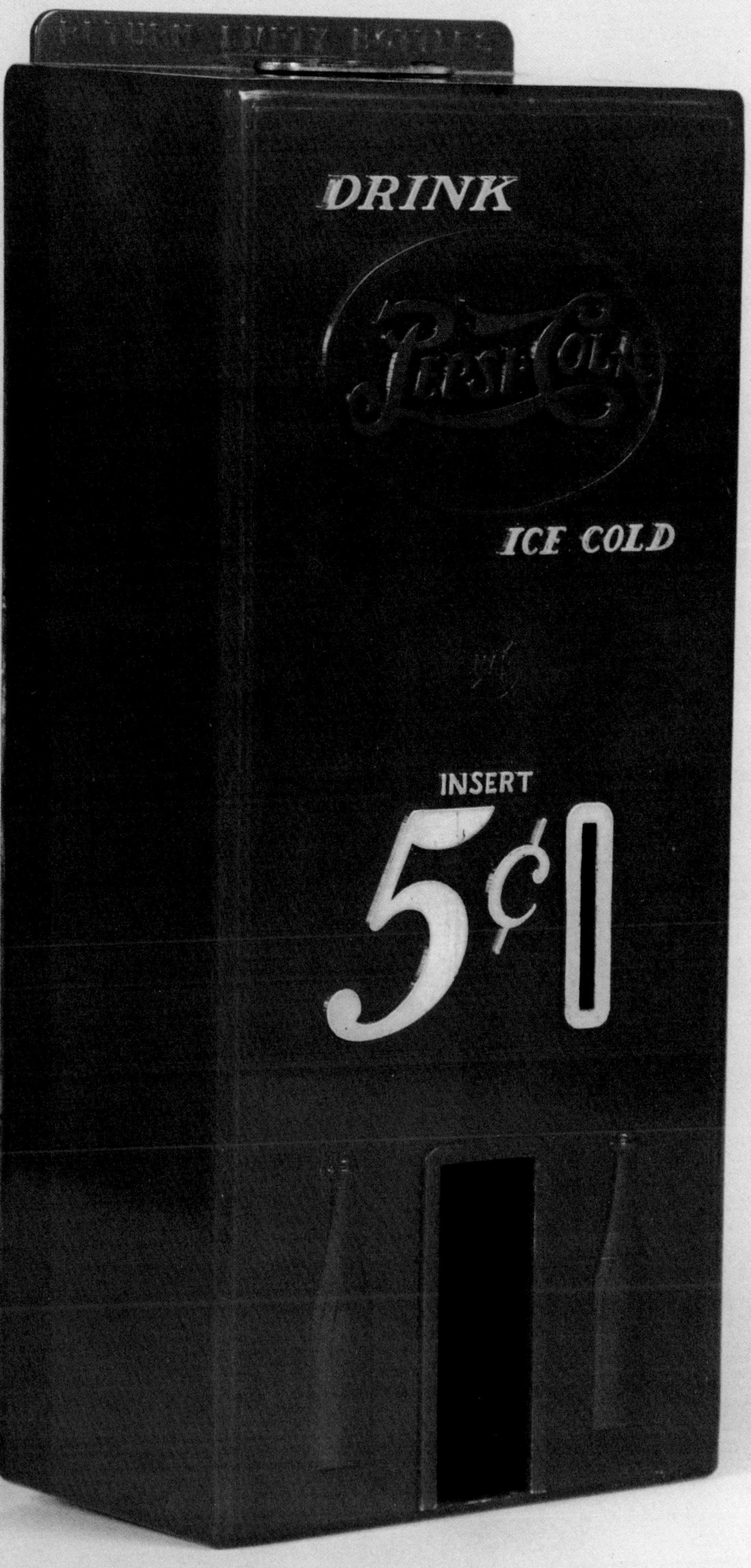
DRINK
Pepsi-Cola
ICE COLD
INSERT
5¢

An Ideal Toys plastic hot-dog wagon with detachable vendor. From the 1940s.

A 1940s wood, masonite, and tin pull-toy from Cass. The bear pedals and rings the bell as the cart is pulled.

A MARX truck with its original box. From the mid-1940s.

From the 1940s or 50s, a white plastic and tin MARX soda truck with miniature Pepsi bottles in cases.

A 1950s tin toy soda truck.

A plastic whistle in the shape of
two Pepsi bottles, from the 1940s
or 1950s.

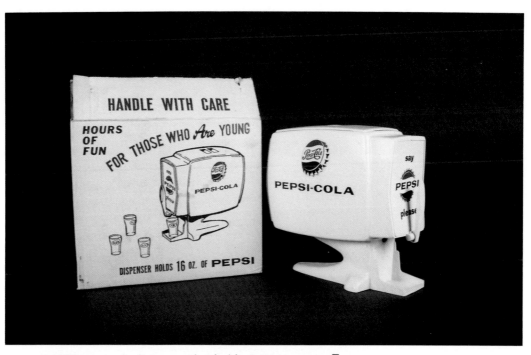

A 1950s toy soda dispenser that holds sixteen ounces. From
Trim Toys.

A 1950s Japanese tin friction soda truck with square tins of Pepsi carried in the back.

From Japan, a 1950s-1960s tin truck with the Pepsi-Cola emblem and bottle on the roof and the Pepsi name on two sides.

A small red 1960s tin-and-plastic soda truck with an open back made in Japan.

Three small steel and plastic toy trucks with Pepsi decals. 1960s.

Two circa-1970 plastic models: a van and a stock car.

Three 1974 Tomica Honda TNIII 360 toy trucks with Pepsi decals.

Two 1978 Tonka soda trucks, one in the original box. Both contain cases of miniature Pepsi bottles.

A yellow plastic Pepsi truck, made in Hong Kong. 1970s.

Two Tyco boxcars in HO scale. From the 1970s.

Lithographed tin. 1961 Ford coupe Pepsi car.

This large ERTL toy truck is from the 1970s.

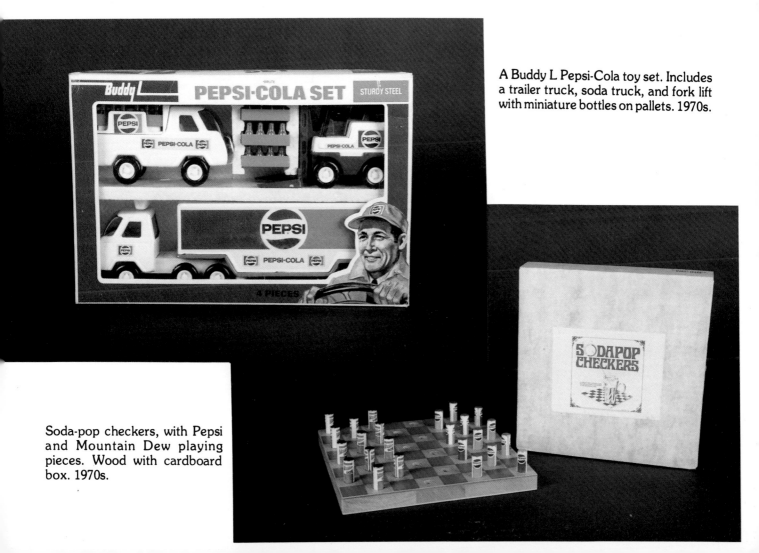

A Buddy L Pepsi-Cola toy set. Includes a trailer truck, soda truck, and fork lift with miniature bottles on pallets. 1970s.

Soda-pop checkers, with Pepsi and Mountain Dew playing pieces. Wood with cardboard box. 1970s.

This large stuffed doll from the 1970s has a Pepsi logo on her winter coat.

A snowman with a Pepsi scarf, hat, and earmuffs. 1970s.

A stuffed Santa from the Trudy Toy Company, Norwalk, Connecticut. He has the Pepsi logo on his belt and is still wearing the original tag. 1970s.

An Animal Fair 1970s Santa with a Pepsi-logo belt buckle. The tag on his left hand reads "Please Hug Me."

Santa and Mrs. Claus sport Pepsi logos. From Animal Fair. 1970s.

An elf and a snowman: small stuffed toys with the Pepsi logo. 1970s.

Chapter XXI
Commemorative Items

A 75th anniversary commemorative combination salt-and-pepper grinder. The box features the image from the 1909 Pepsi calendar.

This replica of the earliest production Pepsi bottle was made for the company's 75th anniversary.

A 1973 Pepsi-can music box commemorating the Pepsi company's 75th anniversary.

A lucite diamond on a felt-covered base marks the 75th anniversary of Pepsi. Produced in conjunction with Walt Disney World and dated October 4, 1972.

A Lenox Commemorative Limited Edition Plate from 1983 features the 1909 Pepsi calendar image.

Chapter XXII

Company Related Items & Awards

Share number one of 150 issued shares of Pepsi-Cola Bottling Company of California stock. Dated 1936.

A letter from Pepsi-Cola Vice president J.W. Pipes dated 9 March 1942.

Dated June 1, 1952, a statement of purpose from the president of Pepsi Cola describing the intended relationship between the bottler and the company.

Pepsi's 1953 Volume Award wood plaque with brass.

The 1953 Per Capita Award wood and brass plaque.

A Pepsi-Cola Award gold bottle with triangular base, from the 1940s.

Chapter **XXIII**

Miscellaneous

 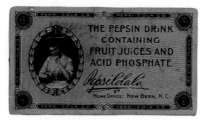

Two sides of a 1908-1909 coupon for one free glass of Pepsi.

A Pepsi bottle deposit ticket from an Ohio grocer.

A postcard, probably from the 1940s, showing a view of Charlotte, North Carolina, that includes a Pepsi-Cola building.

Brass sidewalk markers from the 1920s encourage pedestrians to "Walk safely."